PURPOSEFUL LEADERSHIP

AN INSTRUCTIONAL MANUAL

Kendall Hunt
publishing company

Ramon Tejada

Cover image © Shutterstock, Inc.

www.kendallhunt.com
Send all inquiries to:
4050 Westmark Drive
Dubuque, IA 52004-1840

Published in the United States of America

CONTENTS

ABOUT THE AUTHOR

Courtesy of Ramon Tejada

Ramon Tejada is a faculty member at California State University Channel Islands in Camarillo, California. He teaches Leadership Studies and Kinesiology in the education and liberal studies departments. He has been in leadership roles and in education (teaching, administration, coaching, etc.) for more than 35 years. As a Leadership strategy consultant, Ramon is often asked to assemble teams in organizations in goal and objective productivity for team excellence building. He currently has been working with groups in city and county government agencies in the area of diversity and inclusion in the workplace. Ramon works to achieve competitive greatness and success for companies who are improving on workplace culture while instilling respect, dignity, and quality of life. Ramon has written several articles on leadership (positioning, management, collaboration), and has implemented athletic and movement programs for sport organizations from the college level to the professional ranks. Ramon is currently working on a personal coaching-mentoring model program that will begin instructing and training professional and rising young stars in leadership development in local communities. Ramon's latest publication, "Purposeful Leadership," begins building a leading foundation that pulls out individual leadership traits and characteristics for effective leadership and purposeful spearheading to deliver missioning a vision "fourth quarter" leadership, achieving leadership excellence.

ACKNOWLEDGMENT

To my lovely Wife whose love, passion, and advocacy has paved the way of purposeful leadership in her teaching and for her students.

Our two dazzling daughters who have shown us leadership excellence that is attained through persistence, vision, and independence.

To group Olin, may you all continue the "movement".

INTRODUCTION

"Leadership means Implementation, not Stagnation"

Purposeful leadership is a presentation of oneself to exhibit a process where self-discovery of leading takes shape in a manner of leading skill traits, personal characteristics, and consideration of others.

In building a purposeful leadership platform, a member needs to establish a foundation in steadying a vision of oneself to begin missioning an effective path.

The mission consists of putting a plan of leadership together for executing the fundamentals of who the individual is and what the individual brings to the table.

A leadership plan of success paves the way for the leader to focus on strengths and weaknesses. Here the individual self-realizes what they have as leading skills and what they need to acquire as a balance sheet for leadership.

This Leadership Working Reader and Workbook works to develop and acquire foundational skills and elements for leaders. It delves into the self to realize the essentials needed to be a purposeful leader. In this reader workbook, the individual will build a foundation consisting of self-characteristics in a form of a graphic design symbolizing an image and identity of what they currently are and where they want to be. Their brand will exercise leadership fundamentals by incorporating them into their work and assignments that bring out an understanding of the formation of the role of the leader, practice, and acquire the leadership fundamentals to execute leadership focus.

In Chapter 1, leadership takes on a definition on which the individual begins to build a leadership paradigm. The individual begins a soul-searching process of identifying who they are, identifying what they want to do with leadership, and incorporating approaches in leading for a collective purpose.

In Chapter 2, leading takes on investigating and analyses the platform that is essential for building effective leadership. The crucial components found are communication, decision making, and characteristic sets leading into action. The thought that, "if you are not doing it, some else is," brings about the need to not sit back and make it happen. Being a leader serves a place of life-long learning and contributes to developing and execution of assembling direction.

Chapter 3 examines leadership personalities found in leadership styles and platforms and looks into five leadership examples the author has known and experienced throughout his career and involvement in teaching and leading.

- Authoritative (Setting the tone for direction)
- Mentor (Guidance and support)
- Democratic (Individual and group input)
- Planner (Setting goals, objectives, and end results)
- Coaching (Teaching, modeling, and constructive)

Chapter 4 delves into an understanding of leadership power and leadership common sense. This chapter compares leadership being not a position but rather leadership actions, changes, and implementation. Examination of strategic planning, mind fitness, and environmental awareness supports this challenge of power versus common sense. Creating a grasp of how leadership exercises power to lead and how leadership uses common sense to serve is explored.

In Chapter 5, the discovery of "dealing with the status quo" is assessed through the lens of the individual's view, an affective stance on existence and taking on risk for making change. A process of implementing a vision toward a purposeful mission, and the idea of making it happen to fruition is discussed in this chapter.

Chapter 6 sees the individual as an observant leader. It looks at environmental awareness, being visible, and the need of "being there when you need to BE." Scanning the court opens up an affective venue as to how in touch the individual is with the leading environment.

Chapter 7 assesses the alertness of the individual's preparation and organization to execute. Fourth quarter leadership brings about competitive excellence and effectiveness in knowing success and taking on the unknown, "fear."

CHAPTER 1

A FOUNDATION OF LEADERSHIP

© ksenia_bravo/Shutterstock.com

Leadership takes on a definition: "Leadership" is a process where an individual guides, manages, or supervises a group that involves missioning a vision and undertaking a direction cooperatively toward reaching a collective purpose. The individual begins to build a leadership paradigm, and this paradigm consists of a soul-searching process of identifying who they are, what they want with leadership, and where they want to use it. This leads to creating a leadership foundation for building a personal success plan.

A foundation is defined as a *platform* or *base* for something purposeful. We are familiar with the formation of where a house may be set, but in leadership it begins with where one self's ability and skills are planted for success.

A personal success plan in leadership begins building a foundation with the "self", a soul-searching experience working to develop a plan of leading where one assesses internal and external challenges. Personal leading development brings about enhancing healthy relationships, cohesive teams, and organizations for success.

A leader instills guidance and direction through trust and modeling behavior by, for example, connecting and relating to individuals. The buy-in from an individual or group who is working to reach a collective purpose comes from the leader setting direction with purposeful communication, a well-defined mission, and an enthusiastic approach for leadership delivery.

A cohesive approach in leading infuses formation of a unit that is collectively united for a purposeful direction. Building individual and team cohesiveness results in members knowing what is meant by being part of an interconnected unit. In units such as these, many times members have experienced differentiated network processes that involve a social community; community participation, acquired knowledge in the workplace; worker relations, a notion of unity; personal experience, and the affective sensitivity; how stress and anxiety are handled, etc. These are just some of the cohesive connectors that begin the process that can contribute to unity. Then there is the next question, how are cohesive teams developed? A plan unveiled by the leader paves the way to the mission in for recruiting members to support clarity of the purpose. In this unit, diversity and inclusion add to the support and success of the membership. Leader drives members into the "teamwork mentality" and presents the element of contributing and accepting a role. The opportunity to give input and take input develops communication among the group. In reaching group cohesion, members learn to work together and trust freely in their work tasks.

The author believes there are five building blocks to achieve a collective purpose, and they all present themselves as a process resulting in achieving excellence by (1) showing the way, (2) learning experiences from successes and failures in stimulating the status quo, (3) establishing relationships and networks, seeking a positive outlook for the future, (4) maintaining and gaining an optimistic attitude, enthusiasm, and motivation to grow and develop, and (5) involvement, engagement, and commitment that comes from the soul.

When one accepts a top position, whether head of a company or leading participants for a purpose, it is never simple. When it is laid out clearly, it is a path of true leadership; when it is demonstrated incorrectly, it is called a fiasco. The responsibility points to the individual in a leadership position that has sold trust to the participants that a direction of success will come and involve a team that will thrive and be above all. Leading by example or showing the way demonstrates to individuals or the group that one as a leader can back up their talk, being a person that others want to follow. When a leader talks about doing something and does not complete, it chips away at trust, which is an essential component of leadership.

Individuals in leadership positions create success by showing goodwill and consideration to people. A very productive avenue comes from contributing to the power of believing and buying-into the purposeful direction. It is the leader who initiates firing up the crew, getting others on board, and executing the purposeful mission.

Leading purposefully is achieving excellence by being true to your mission, to yourself, and the purpose. Executing ground rules for paving the direction for a straight-up leader is to model the right example by being assertive in acting the part by taking charge and talking about what you know. Be willing to take responsibility and not blame others, and put the group first, give acknowledgement to the ones in the trenches.

For purposeful leadership to become high achieving it must have competency in the areas of strategic planning and competitive excellence. To be successful at this, the individual needs to have experiences in wins and losses, learning from successes and failures. Strategic planning is an efficient way to solve problems, while competitive excellence is taking on an issue with preparation and being well organized.

Experiencing failure presents a negative outlook toward a purposeful plan that may not want to embrace this idea of failure learning. Failure has always been looked and felt as an empty fulfillment. But failure can be a great teacher and it is just that "failure recovery" is difficult to overcome. It is how we interpret failure and turn it into teaching moments to push forward. We need to think about understanding teaching moments to change and improve our efforts because "efforts" are ways of energizing ourselves to develop and move forward. Considering pushing failure to the side can be rethinking your planning and preparation and your strategy of executing redirection and working to control what you are able to manage and letting go of what you realize you have no control over.

Successful learning can be a learning tool where one obtains benefits of learning from success rather than enjoying success. Success learning is a practice of a learning dynamic for continuous progression toward success. Enjoying success is short term and may develop into a state of complacency. Success needs to be a reminder of how hard it was to achieve it. Careful planning, strategic thinking, trial and error, and, ultimately, hard work cannot be substituted. Keep in mind success renders the saying, "You are only as good as your last win," meaning you can experience success, but success should have a steady focus and innovation for ongoing challenges and changing environments, cultures, and communities.

It is important to make good relations at work, in a group, and all around you. It brings a feeling of participation and team moving toward a productive state. A good relationship considers trust as a trait where honesty fosters communication and an effective work environment. Another one is honoring respect, by accepting people's input and valuing their contributions. Inclusion and diversity are two more elements that support differences in the group environment that can lead to building external and internal feeling for establishing networks and relations.

Your leadership foundation should incorporate relationships and networks, seeking a positive outlook for a purposeful future. A road map to acquiring these elements of connectivity is to not underestimate or hold back on relationships and contacts that come from adjacent industry or within your work environment on getting the know how to or update useful information for success. A scouting report on potential network candidates needs to create an area of commonality to open up shared interests to form relationships. Learn to expect nothing in return but be interested and helpful to work on the relationships. Show your confidence when dealing with potential relationships that add to your network. Have no fear, reach high, and make yourself humble in connecting to an opportunity that can bring in others in building the network environment. In all, I believe that networking is like a tree, developing short branches and long branches. But each branch grows a branch within itself to spread, reach, and support the tree whose foundation is planted firmly.

Networking contributions from individuals practicing leadership enable them to become potential recruits for institutions, companies, and organizations. It is the success of these leaders that bring productive skills for success at delivering ideas and innovation for leadership change.

Exploring and finding leadership skills and ideas may be hidden within the individual's emergence to show what their abilities and capabilities may be. This can begin with developing a personal plan of success where the individual seeks to self-realize the inner leadership traits that can be released through this personal success plan. It is crucial in leadership that the individual learn about themselves. Taking on a leadership direction where influencing others and accepting a purposeful direction is no joke and needs to be taken serious because it involves working with people.

As we end this chapter, the student will begin to think about their leadership paradigm and develop a plan of success that mirrors their abilities, skills, feelings, purpose for working with people and setting the foundation for missioning a vision. This application exercise involves developing a graphic symbolization (pyramid) of discovering you as the leader within.

WORKSHEET #1

Directions: Create your plan of success. Include what you feel mirrors your abilities, skills, feelings, purpose for working with people, and setting foundation for missioning a vision for purposeful leadership. Also, define leadership, your definition, what you feel it means?

PLAN OF SUCCESS

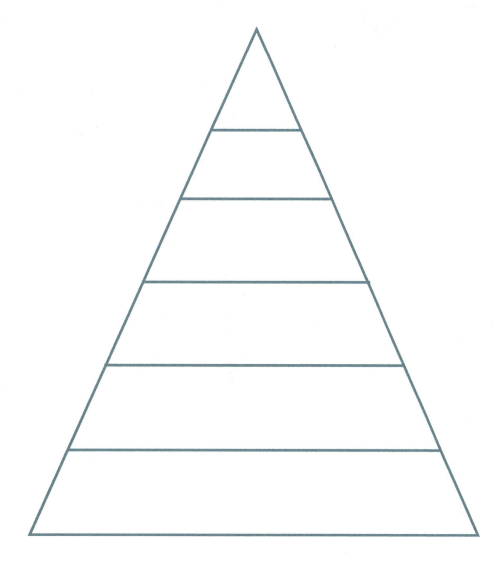

WORKSHEET #2

Defining **Your** Leadership Platform.

Define Leadership _____

_____.

Place a leadership characteristic in each tier level in your plan of success and define it.

1.

2.

3.

4.

5.

6.

WORKSHEET #3

Write a one page reflection on your leadership paradigm.

I believe that leadership should benefit the group's interests, and the well-being of the whole group, as a collective. Decisions should be made with everyone in mind, not just the person in the formal "leader" role. It's should be a team effort. Also, even if there is a designated "leader," leadership should be shared, so there isn't just one person/ruler overpowering everyone else. Additionally, along those same lines, leadership should be inclusive and promote diversity. On top of that, I think leadership should be flexible and open to change. In other words, it is important to take risks and be willing to adapt where necessary. Basically, I think my leadership paradigm involves shared leadership, where everyone pitches in the work toward common goals and [illegible]. Everyone works together and makes decisions together to benefit the whole team. Multiple perspectives are taken into account.

CHAPTER 2

ESSENTIALS OF BUILDING LEADERSHIP

© Andrew Paul Deer/Shutterstock.com

Leading takes on investigating and analyzing the leadership platform that is essential for the start of building effective leadership. Crucial components are found in communication, decision making, and characteristic sets of leadership action. The thought that, "if you are not doing it, some else is," brings about the need to not sit back and make it happen. Being a leader serves a place of life-long learning and contributes to developing and execution of purposeful direction.

Effective leadership steadies itself on a leadership platform that self-investigates and self-analyzes the true formation of a leader. This platform serves as a set of beliefs that will develop the individual for what they will be identified as. This platform energizes the mission and vision of the organization. It is here that the individual will pull out a purposeful direction that will lead the organization and place responsibility upon the leader.

A leadership platform is established by communicating your foundation and purpose to the group or organization that you will be working with. Also, your contribution of the ideals that you may want to leave as a leader will mark your time while you were at the helm. Your reflection of the time you were at the helm will connect you to what you did, and how you did it will say a lot of who you are.

Individuals in positions of leadership are examined by the importance they give to issues, and the time it takes to address them. The behavior on how you deal with matters delivers the message to people that you are a leader that takes importance as a priority. Many times, this can be a form of how people hold your leading ability as accountability. This can be a good way to measure results from your contributory status.

Some platform ideals can be associated with the way that you promote a safe climate in the workplace. People are very productive when they feel safe and their workplace location is supported. It is crucial for inclusion and diversity to live in the workplace and with coworkers that all are respected and human dignity is honored. Remember, the people in the trenches are the ones who drive production with leadership that has a genuine consideration for their expertise and experience.

Sound leadership ideas need to be purposeful in its message. It shows up the delivery of communication, and on how decision making impacts and supports innovation. Measuring character by these ideals above provides an organization's development into a changing environment that workplace participants can be part of and contributes with ownership.

The leadership platform needs to be of preparation and organization. Ideals that are purposeful and conveyed to the group or organization need to be researched and concluded with a plan and response; basically, do your homework. The leadership platform serves as a position, "where you stand," enabling your purpose to advance, measure your results, and the industriousness of your group or organization.

There are components of leadership that support your platform, and you need to establish these in your plan of success. These components will set your lead into action and will begin to shape you and your purpose.

Some leadership components need to fit the individual, and others may need to be developed through experience. Leadership practices add to the leadership platform for effective delivery of purposeful leadership.

In order for the leadership to be purposeful, it needs to be supported by foundational components for an effective delivery. Leadership effectiveness means believing, trusting, and having confidence in the organization's goals that include workplace satisfaction and the safe conditions for people who are the contributors to the organization. Another is, "communication." This needs to be provided by the leadership involving the workplace participants in missioning the vision of the organization with a purposeful focus that conveys the strategy, making them part of executing the objectives of the organization for attainment, resulting in group participation for the benefit of all.

Effectiveness in leadership should inspire the organization to continue to offer training and development from the administration level down to the workforce levels. "An individual", is given the opportunity to improve value sets into participant confidence and productive levels of giving and working alignments. Showing value and respect to employees is a component needed for effective leading that cashes in on personal fulfillment and setting higher goals for themselves.

Leadership is a life-long learning that serves as a continuum for the development of the self. Keeping up in the 21st century brings about the needs that evaluate our ability to adjust in our thinking ways, how we learn, and our relationships that we build. Those in leadership positions need to focus on becoming up-to-date on world movement. Leaders who are aware of social change and look to re-vent their environment are open and develop a yearning to keeping active. Leaders accept responsibilities that capture a view that will enhance the significance of their groups and organization.

The global market today is stimulated by the way an innovative economy is inspired by its resources. But the way the networking aspect connects to this world market is seen as a learning skill, being a constant changer and influence. Therefore, leadership needs to foster learning and be significant of self-development in leading learning for change. The methods to the madness of dealing with issues and problems are to head them with innovation. If we look at our work environment as a learning place and the opportunity to learn at work as we exercise our work tasks, then those in leadership positions need to empower learning.

Developing a competitive edge for individuals comes out of knowing how relationships are assembled. The information learned from connecting with people and the reflections that come out of human interactions add experience to individuals in developing awareness. To assist leadership learning, a program should be available where participants can master and acquire personal knowledge for a life-long learning plan. This plan for individuals needs to possess professional development by a program that looks to discover, communicate, decision making, and collaboration.

Discovery lends itself to researching new ideas and staying up-to-par on current events. Globally, information is widespread in many facets of our world. We learn and develop how to make sense of the information in our environment. It is essential to assess and measure the network of information by collecting the results to make them comprehensible to our existence and the way we work. What is most important is communicating through networks and relationships that participants form to assist in guiding the information accumulated that serves to impact the way we see things. Decision making is how we brand information and delivers it for acting on solid ideas for clearing the way for achieving goals and objectives for purpose.

Decision making comprises reflecting and placing ideas into practice as we learn. It works to support critical thinking as well as organize our thinking experiences, images, and emotions. Collaboration gathers networking resources, ideas, and experiences with our teams and workplace participants. Collaboration supports a process of moving acquired information to all while learning and reflecting together. We form respect and trust by making things real by using social and work networks.

By discovery, decision making, and collaboration, participants in an organization learn together in a process where acquisition of skills, networking, and new ideas are brought forward to enhance developmental leadership.

In developing and executing an organization's strategic plan, leading an effective and purposeful direction needs to be real and attainable. Identify on how you will bring communication issues and tasks to the table. Many times, communication is sent out, and it is not aligned to the direction for the needed outcome. Set your different levels for employees and give them the preparation and tools needed to participate effectively to execute the tasks. Set the goals and objectives by clearly stating a purposeful direction for each level of workforce production. The engagement process from the workforce needs clear information that is assessable for all levels of employee teams that are involved. It is here that levels of communication are consistent, have clarity for task completion, and keep people on the same page. Remember to consider state-of-the-art technology. Media and tech platforms that are familiar to workers need to be provided to develop the support area and bring about a motivation and an enthusiastic attitude to task performance. This contribution of worker participation sets the line for productivity that assembles direction and executes the fundaments for task completion.

In leadership, the need to set a course for visualization and purpose is always in need of a plan. An effective strategic planning structure is one of the highest responsibility that needs to be presented by the one in charge. Individuals and groups look to see where the organization is going and wants to know how it will be sustainable and successful. This workplace etching needs to be clear, or the focus may be lost in not fulfilling the purposeful direction.

When individuals and groups see the direction well defined and comprehensible, then all begin to bond up. The plan becomes an effective purpose that is seen to support sustainment and future success. This plan or purpose creates expectations that all will set to fulfill from the administrators down to the workplace environment and its participants. It is these tasks that will be outlined for all to follow and check off as momentum turns into action.

A planning system must be made a priority and agreed upon by all stakeholders that commitment is at hand. The plan whether short or long needs to be visited each year and see if adjustments need to be made. This is a good way to keep new ideas and adjustments of the plan alive and aligned to what has been approved. As always, leadership needs to make sure and stay committed to the plan and any adjustments that are made.

To structure and support this strategic plan for action, there are components that need to be effectively recognized in order to answer its purpose. The purpose may go into asking the why's and what's of its start to action. The next one should be best practices or core values that instill priority and the will to stick to a foundation that will direct beliefs for all to follow. As always, a missioning vision that is purposeful sets long-term yearly goals to keep all on task. There should be an outline or agenda setting all topics and projects that will lead the individual or group into a directive mode.

The components of a strategic plan are crucial in executing effective planning and leadership purpose. The roles that are carried out from administrators down to the workforce need to be defined in order to complete the distribution of labor and its purposeful contribution. This in turn leads to sustainability and success for the goals and objectives of the organization to execute and complete.

Strategic planning needs to be the tone setter for an organization. It is the blueprint of what it wants to accomplish and adhere to for an organization. It is a foundation for the workplace participants and leadership to continue to collaborate and plan. The bottom line, an effective strategic plan keeps the possibility for transparency and accountability to sustain boundaries for a successful outcome for an organization.

WORKSHEET #4

Select and reflect on a leader that demonstrates two essential leadership skills: Communication and decision making. Write a one page summary discussing how a leader uses communication effectively and the decision making process to consider everyone and everything in a leadership position.

_____ great
Co_____ and decision _____ skills
is on___ ___ supervisors at ___ ___ _____
for __ __ ___ mentor. My supervisor
Cristina __ communicates with me and
___ _____ __. Meeting is on __ thing
important to ___ ____. She does this both
in person during team meetings and also
via e-mail ___ ___ ___. __ ___ ____ questions
that she must know __ ___ ___ ___ ___ the
top of her head. She make__ sure to follow
up with me as soon as possible. I have
also noticed that she makes __ ___ in a
way that includes and acknowledges the ___ ___tives
of the whole team. She makes sure all ___
our voices are heard and our opinions are
accounted for. For example, ___ __ ___ ___ are
willing to think of ways to recruit new hires
for next year, and at our most recent
team meeting my supervisor broke us into
smaller groups to brainstorm and ___ everyone
to share their ideas.

WORKSHEET #5

Leadership Communication Skills Survey

For each question, underline the answer that you most closely connect to in action, thought, or decision in each situation:

Q1. When speaking to workplace participation about a significant upcoming change in the workplace environment, how would you address this?

Send out a global e-mail

Set up a department meeting with department heads

Just make the change

Q2. When giving feedback, how would you address this?

Give them what you think will close a short specific meeting on what was done well

Just say "Nice job," and appreciate it

Share a note of commendation that will go into their file, on their evaluation, and show appreciation

Q3. When an employee gets emotional (upset, angry, etc.), how would you handle it?

Send the employee home for the day

Listen to what is bothering them

Tell them that showing emotions in the workplace is not acceptable

Q4. When you need to make a crucial decision that affects employees and the organization, you would do:

Trust your experience and gut

Take a good look at risk factors

Assess options against company values, vision, and mission to check alignment of strategic purpose

Q5. The relationship that links communication to strategy, and culture is:

There is no relationship among these three

Communication connects all three together

The organizational culture must be there before good communication or a strategic plan

CHAPTER 3
LEADERSHIP PLATFORMS

© Steve Boice/Shutterstock.com

This chapter examines leadership personalities found in leadership styles and looks into five leadership platforms the author has known and experienced throughout his career and involvement in teaching and leading. Here the leadership styles are identified as being authoritative, mentoring, planning, coaching, and democratic.

We look at leadership styles as paving a direction, planning, and strategies for inspiring teams and individuals. Every leader works to acquire a unique groundbreaking style in working, managing, and leading individuals. Beginning out of the areas of hiring and a supervisory perspective, encountering the challenges of single leadership styles can be advantageous in positioning leaders within the workplace. When choosing leaders that fit the right position, the focus should examine how the goals and strategic objectives for the organization reach attainment.

To understand a leadership style is to know strengths and weaknesses in the area of leading. One needs to be active and purposeful as a leader by tactically exercising strengths and offsetting weak areas. One's leadership platform should describe the values and morals that will support communication within the work environment and its participants. As the word out there says, "knowing is strength." One should always prepare to advance and move forward in job-seeking opportunities by the knowledge, experience, and education development that supports the leader to perform. The authoritative style provides a direction and attempts to lead the way for individuals, groups, and organizations that need to improve productivity and purpose for success. Sometimes the direction can be my way or the highway, as it is often said to avoid barriers. Truly, this style of leading sets tone for the road ahead.

Authoritative ways will develop goals and objectives but gives room for team members to provide input as to how they are going to arrive at their goals. Authoritative approaches labor well when the team needs a purposeful mission that creates a vision, where members can be self-disciplined enough to solve how to achieve a successful path.

In need of motivating individuals and groups, an authoritative style can bring a feeling of optimistic and assured leadership into a work environment. This lead style can stimulate and encourage workplace participants to believe in the purpose and take on a productive and positive attitude. Authoritative leaders will attempt to motivate participants in addressing the created goals and objectives put forth by the group in developing a planned direction, positive input, and an environment where teamwork can commence productivity. This style is strategic when, beginning a new direction or project, placing new goals and objectives that are achievable and direct to go after the purposeful outcome.

When we speak of work and leadership relationships, often the style of leading called mentoring is one that guides and supports in the work environment. Mentoring looks at establishing relationships and really does not look at performance. Mentors take on assigned mentees that are potential work participants for leading and instilling knowledge, awareness, and individual experiences. Because of these mentoring elements, the mentee learns to acquire skills and actions for improving on the job awareness and begins a developmental process that will gain support and leadership. At the same time, mentees can learn to feel open to ask questions, seek references to issues, express themselves, and share ideas.

The concept of effective relationships between the mentor and mentee lies in the area of development for improvement. Leadership with mentees becomes purposeful in trusting a guiding hand and having a confidant for self-growth and professional development. With the young workforce coming into organizations and the job market, the worthiness of advice and experience can set a foundation for exposure in leadership development. Forming skill incentives and attainment move to create a mentor–mentee relationship because both parties look at the relationship to be purposeful. Individuals who plan to stay employed and vested tend to seek direction from mentors to help them keep building connections to their work assignment and for professional progression.

A democratic leader exhibits participation from all individuals and groups for input that will contribute to talking up and sharing ideas for organizational communication and innovation. It encourages all to share thoughts that move a project forward to tackle new areas of venturing. Participation is big in this leadership style as it merits the contribution from members and peers. Even though leader head makes the final decision, involvement is essential for cohesive group building. The team attitude and voice contribute to the decision process by adding input in a manner that builds a sense of ownership and value. Keeping work participants engaged, having them know they are in the loop, and knowing changes that can occur keep their part in the participatory process transparent.

In leadership, preparation and organization are two elements that are essential for gaining a reputation for being dependable and reliable. The leader name given to this type of individual is sometimes known as "a leadership planner." A leadership planner is strong in getting matters completed but can also be the voice of reason by being the force in the room.

A planner by leadership identification leads by setting visual goals, having clear objectives, and communicating in a comprehensible manner. One places expectations so that individuals know how to approach you as a leader rather than being quiet and nonconnected. This lead approach wants to place people at comfort level. The organizational premise and the preparation this lead style exhibits is to demonstrate ability and knowledge building value in confidence and readiness showing orderliness to the group. The planner displays a humble side to delivery and the discipline thats needed to build trustworthy directives for working with individuals and groups. This manner of leading can have quick and positive results because of the way participants respond to orders for completing assigned work tasks. Concise directives are straight and clear to complete because a planner does not accept detouring from the goal. The primary driver of this leading style is concretely keeping all in order and that the team seeks goal completion. The planner values structure and stability for success that is purposeful for attainment. Understand that results-oriented leaders (planners) always have their eyes on the prize. Although, scheduled to conceive purpose, to planners, getting in the way or disrupting the goal looks as losing focus. Leadership planning works to steady the vision not to be stuck in the forest but to be able to walk through it and capture the light.

Many times, in the leadership arena, an organization and workforce participants need a coach. We have experienced many individuals throughout our education journey that have served that role.

Coaching as a leadership style shapes itself as an individual that teaches and models best practices, is constructive, and instills training techniques for development in the work environment and individual preparedness.

A leader who possesses coaching abilities shows strength to work participants and group development. Coaches concern themselves on being effective with the time capsule available to assist, work with the work environment and participants in identifying and advancing individual areas of professional strength. The coach delivers constructive criticism, poses advice, and teaches by example modeling. The coaching method supports organizations in assessing and developing raw young talent. Forecasting new technologies and using methodologies that challenge the status quo for improving operations and best practices for all bring about workplace changes as the coach guides and directs purposeful learning. Coaching contributes to competitive significance for helping employees improve their work practices for professional development and individual effectiveness. Coaches emphasize action and delivery for work participants to be at their greatest level when they asked to demonstrate level greatness. Organizational leaders should be coached up to perform and think for themselves placing accountability and transparency for their decisions and an effective skill set development that supports purposeful plans.

In a leadership summation, the author concludes that all leaders come in different sizes, colors, personalities, specific agendas, philosophies, experiences, positional fits, and background knowledge.

One thing to understand in leadership styles is that leaders exhibit the ability to adjust to the situations and challenges to address expertise and effectiveness for the purpose at hand. Remember, there are diverse personalities, positional roles, and experience that come into play for leaders to solve the issues. Leadership styles sometimes do not match all acts of leading, but avoiding a style works and the fact that some styles may overlap each other can be appropriate for behaviors and purpose. The leadership style comes into play as the situation presents itself. Sometimes the nature of the lead style has to do with the need of the organization of the job at hand. There may be exceptions to the rule but some leadership styles innately match with specific professional segments, as other leading styles may not.

WORKSHEET #6

Do you know your leadership style?

Instructions

For each question, select A, B, or C. Your answers should be in your real time.

Answer 12 Questions	A	B	C
1. A serious issue within my team: (A) I review that we have goals to accomplish. (B) Assemble my team and open discussion on the issue. (C) I let them work independently for individual space empowerment.	☐	☐	☐
2. I have faith and trust in my team participants: (A) A lot. (B) Some-what. (C) Do not depend on them.	☑	☐	☐
3. Some of my team members are skilled and driven. Team: (A) Are free to create and research. (B) Have input and organizational meeting with me. (C) Everyone follows same workplace tactics and practices.	☐	☑	☐
4. My effective method in evaluating my team is executing best results by (A) Standing and Leading. (B) Motivating all team members to be participatory. (C) Delegate projects and assignments to everyone.	☐	☐	☑
5. A deadline of one day for a job that I feel needs two days: (A) I communicate the deadline and send everyone to get on it. Trust them and don't worry that they will get the task done on time. (B) Meet my team and get input on how to meet the deadline. (C) Send out instructions to each team member to finish job on time.	☐	☐	☐
6. Low-performance worker should be (A) disciplined, so not to repeat. (B) Meet and speak with individual, to explain best practices. (C) Don't address it.	☐	☑	☐

7. I will implement new social media and pro-graming strategies, I will: (A) Present the plan myself and then sell it to the team. (B) Have meeting with team for information and input. (C) Delegate the task to team for solution.	☐	☑	☐
8. I let my team: (A) Problem solve. (B) Meet and come up with ideas and bring a decision to me. (C) Meet with me to communicate how I want the job to look.	☐	☑	☐
9. I have a new member on my team: (A) I let her/him find the best way to complete tasks. (B) I involve individuals into team information-al meetings. (C) Meet with individuals until they understand practices and the values of our team excellence.	☐	☐	☑
10. Effective leaders: (A) Use the best methods. (B) Communicate and consider best practic-es for team success. (C) Let team members work independently.	☐	☑	☐
11. When asked if you are a team builder: (A) Not confident. (B) Yes. (C) Look bewildered.	☐	☑	☐
12. What do I do when my team members look dejected, I: (A) look into her/his work produc-tion and see if he/she is addressing his/her tasks. (B) Ensure that he/she is an active team member participant and contributing. (C) Leave it alone and see where this goes.	☐	☑	☐

CHAPTER 4
POWER VERSUS COMMON SENSE

© alberto clemares exposito/Shutterstock.com

This chapter involves leadership as not a position but rather leadership actions, changes, and implementation. Examination of strategic planning, mental fitness, and alertness in leading will show support for exercising the challenges in equating power versus common sense in the leading area. Creating a grasp of how leadership applies the ability to lead and how command uses common sense to serve looks at best practices for leadership effectiveness.

Power in the leadership world interprets various ways in exercising the property of headship. It is used in many facets in the leading arena, appropriately and inappropriately. An understanding of power in leading stands for measuring an asset and making a call on a particular thing while enforcing it. Defining power can be interpretive but let us look at it as meaning the capacity to direct or influence the conduct of others or the course of events. A prepared leader can exercise power in various ways. It is how careful and considerate that the power-vested individuals and events be prepared and organized. An organization works to secure their interests. Individuals and events are merely assets that find a fit for use in an organization for executing excellence. Power is a display of an authoritative exercise in making decisions and dealing with people. The critical part of power here is to use it efficiently and patiently for strong power enforcement. It has always been that power looks like a superior way of using it compared to possessing it to achieve excellent results. Understanding power and using it for a directive causes misunderstandings to parties who receive duties, whether on the positive or the negative side. This is where common sense plays a form of accountability for measuring decisions. Research and preparation can render a well-organized outcome when common sense is involved keeping an order of mental fitness balanced between power and common sense. A definition of common sense is good sense and sound judgment.

Common sense serves to deliver practical decisions that deal with daily matters. The art of incorporating common sense into the leadership arena works to understand and make sense by all. Understanding common sense each day brings about a human trait that develops a purposeful awareness that needs discipline.

Individuals need to use common sense in the workplace for challenges that require preparation for sound decision making that could be seen as being wise. A leader learns from personal experiences and should be real in humbling sensitivity in serving consequences. Leaders need to be reasonable and have the excellent understanding to do the right thing for situations and conflicts. They should know the difference between being responsible and irresponsible. Many times, leaders need to act on intellect and not on emotion. But some may have a weakness here, but it is never too late to improve and acquire common sense.

Understanding leadership looks at power versus common sense affecting decisions and positional leveraging. Often, it is the tone that sets the treatment of individuals that forms foundational outcomes. It could be said that maybe these outcomes reflect changes and circumstances that all see as setting precedence. Organizational challenges could also be formable among decision results and outcomes. Leaders who exercise power could begin to develop a culture of establishing policy favoring their influence of procedures. Common sense leading is essential here because it considers individuals and workplace productivity to represent a whole organization versus a sole proprietor of driving for self-preservation.

This concept of dealing with power versus common sense as a leader propels a realization that headship is not a position but rather a platform for exercising purposeful actions of support and missioning a vision for leadership effectiveness.

In the field of leadership followers who stand behind a leader and for a purpose want to accomplish tasks for a change. It is true that leadership styles that drive organizational needs and workforce production wish to be productive and successful. But the idea of cohesiveness and collaboration go a long way when contributory participants striving to be proactive in making action consistently and adding to attaining goals and strategical margins can impede progress.

The fact that power versus common sense affects outcomes of changes and implementation in areas that are recommended for attainment may show lack of trust.

Leaders move people to bring out the best in them. A quick definition of leadership is influencing a group of people toward achieving common organizational goals. The conduct of a leader, the style that is used to implement change, and work outcomes result in tasking for completion and hopefully fulfillment. Effective decision making is vital to your people and organizational success.

Decision making is the practice of making choices by pinpointing sources, collecting data, and evaluating supportive approaches. A strategic plan involving the decision-making process can be measured using identified decisions by purposeful data information and pinpointing the direction.

Sound and purposeful decisions qualify support to lead the life you want. Focused decision-makers are needed in the workplace and can contribute their skills to excel in their career. Therefore, it is crucial that balancing power and common sense make effective decisions for a purposeful work environment and organizational prowess.

It is helpful in adding five significant steps to balancing power and using common sense to make effective decisions.

In the following table decision making is set in a sequence to consider:

Identify the goal	Be innovative and visionary
Gather data	Preparation
Think about the outcomes	Check for understanding
Exercise the decision	Take responsibility
Assess decision	Evaluate change effectiveness

Making good decisions is a quality that will help you lead the life you want. Good decision-makers need to be active in their work environment and demonstrate their skills to develop and enhance their position and work relationships.

Seek purposeful outcomes	
Be independent	
Turn your brain off	
Don't problem solve, decide	
Admit your mistakes	

Steps for a sound and effective decision:

Zoom in on objectives and goals	
Do your research	
Input from your team	
Chances/risks	
Pros and cons	

The choices and decisions one makes are a part of life. Life evolves, with ups and downs, involving us to make choices and decisions through our span of development. It is so fascinating and somewhat perplexing that by the time young people have reached adulthood many have not attained the skills of decision making. It is a stone fact; many people are slow to change because this takes them out of their comfort level.

There is a reason for decisions to open a dialogue on why some people can throw themselves into living life and do it with free-wheeling enthusiasm and eagerness, while others overthink at having to do anything that might need purpose and out of the status quo arena. An individual's attitude contributes to the way they look at living life. As few people are unafraid, anxiety-free, and adventurous, others have fear, being the unknown/unfamiliar to reach high. Sometimes lacking experience which reflects one's power and common sense can unbalance limits in their position.

Decision making is something we all need to learn how to do and how to apply it to our lives. Life skills need learning from day one since decision making gathers experience practice to master. Excellent choices and decisions of wisdom come out of several factors: (1) stage of life, (2) ideas of right and wrong, (3) understanding that the decision-making process entails learning and acquiring experience, and practice.

The realization of decision making needs to lend itself to exercising power to make things happen, "the old dropping the hammer." But on the other side, ordinary sense serving accountability can be an equalizer for purposeful decisions.

WORKSHEET #7

Leadership Decision-Making Scenarios

Please address each <u>Scenarios</u> with your solution.

Scenario 1: Delegate everything that someone else can do.

Scenario 2: Travel to your employees rather than requiring them to come to you.

Scenario 3: Share your information with you team.

Scenario 4: Take the same pay raise as your employees.

Scenario 5: Do you have open door policy, yes or no, why?

[Handwritten responses — partially legible:]

Scenario 1: Consider the strengths of everyone on the team, then delegate / assign tasks according to individual strengths and weaknesses.

Scenario 2: My solution → If there is a great distance between my employees and me, we could save travel time and meet on Zoom instead (remotely). Or if in-person is preferred, we could meet in the middle.

Scenario 3: I'm not sure if this means contact information, but if it does, my solution would be to only share a work email or phone number to give myself time/privacy and not let work interfere with my personal life.

Scenario 4: I would only take the same
pay raise as my employees
if I felt that it was fair
to. If someone does something
extra remarkable to make them
stand out, they should be
recognized accordingly, so in
cases like that, they should
get a bigger raise.

Scenario 5: I do have an open-door policy because
I think everyone has value and
their ideas should be taken into
consideration. I enjoy getting to
know different perspectives because
I believe everyone has something
unique to offer. I also want
people to know that I am
approachable, and that they should
feel free to come to me with
any questions or concerns they
may have. Above all, I aim
for transparency because I
believe it builds trust.

Scenario 4: I would only take the same
pay raise as my employees

CHAPTER 5
DEALING WITH THE STATUS QUO

© Kit Korzun/Shutterstock.com

The discovery of "dealing with the status quo" is assessed through the lens of the individual's view and practical stance on the existence or taking on risk for making the change. The process of vision, application towards mission attainment, and the idea of making it happen to fruition look at testing leadership as a game changer.

Status quo comes from the Latin expression signifying the present state of concerns that focuses on social, political, and human matters. Looking at societal senses, it relates to keeping pace or transforming society's organizations and ideas that are in place. The status quo lives on keeping things the way it is.

In challenging the status quo, individuals need to pace themselves in taking on actions or disruptions at a pace. When individuals dare decisions and actions, risk can be fearless, discovery and exploratory avenues open up, and risk into reward, and fear into purpose can change. Adding to challenging the status quo, will result in detecting innovative ideas and purposeful methods for missioning your goals, the workplace environment, and peer networking and presenting the organization's potential assets on the table. Networking contributes value and ownership for success.

In leadership, purposeful causes and organizations that want to be productive with change and succeed at what they set up need to challenge the status quo. Leaders test the status quo to make the difference, whether in social or organizational settings. Organizations question the status quo on making improvements for directional and strategical transformation. People will take on the status quo for personal development and career enhancement.

Dealing with the status quo from the lens of the individual's view ponders inquiry into a transformative process. This process unveils possibilities that seek purposeful thinking in implementation and adjustments for the need to place the status quo on trial. Many times, the expectations and the learning discovery resulting from adjustments of action brings about the thinking of, "looking at both sides of the coin." The idea of looking at both sides of the coin shows on one side, what it is and on the other side, what it could be. When dealing with the status quo, our skills are put on the line, and we bring about how to look at possibilities in a different light for the purpose. The notion of contention freezes momentum to expand. In the workplace environment, it should be a place that sets climate to do better, to share diversity for empowerment, and call out the leadership to be hands-on to invent and commit to shaking up the "same mo, same mo." This obligation places inspiration on a tray to take and consume purposeful thinking and product advancement.

In approaching change and making it happen in a purposeful direction, establishing a scaffold of ideas to follow can be a direction for the purposeful change of sequences to follow.

Employees see change when the management supports directions displayed by the workforce. It is crucial when management demonstrates encouragement for changes and validates the communication process and the visibility it shows to interact and be approachable. One error that often occurs with control is conveying mixed messages or flip-flopping. Do not commit to a change endeavor if you as a leader cannot sustain it; this will cause a downfall in your leadership strength.

Change can be challenging for a purposeful measure and an idea of how to present it. A paradigm for change comes about from many sources and incidents. It results from dissatisfactory information that comes from employees, company surveys, and lack of goals and objectives for a purposeful scheme. Today's world preys on considering data as being a reliable indicator to detect capacities that need to improve change. An area of active consideration for change happens when management involves the workforce in the process of engagement. Adding organizational change, for example, has to include clarity and communication that is intentional to change. Specifically, changes will influence the workplace climate, the production environment, and security for employee positions.

A winner in leading is to be transparent with employees and welcome input from the participants, which can benefit the planning and implementation for effectiveness. The key here is the workforce, which is close to the processes in the work environment and the need to know what is coming down the pike to purpose and contributing to the change. When a leader becomes a communicator in making the change, being prepared and organized for structuring a plan of transparency and purposeful relations shows stability. The stain of being a poor communicator and, "here say," information can build negative attitudes toward change. Leadership needs to be proactive in communication and for system effectiveness to recruit the workplace participants to feel ownership.

In proposing the change, excellent communication is about the reeling out and executing ideas of evolution. A positive focus on instilling a strategic plan to implement and for change needs goals and objectives that drive process change and keeps workforce participants in the loop. For example, if an organization is developing a new training program for employee development, it should set up a task force representing areas of the workers, managers, and the administration. A strategic plan will permit time, input, and including the organization's mission for implementation to commence. Again, excellent communication and transparency keep a dialogue open and eliminate confusion as to the purpose and direction of the process.

Whenever a change is made, a change assessment model needs to evaluate the progress and existing results from the plan of goals and objectives that were set up. Sometimes an adjustment on the focus needs to keep momentum steady for best results toward a continuum for forwarding movement. Sometimes plans meet barriers when applying changes. This of course, depends on how these barriers are addressed to overcome delays and disappointment. It is management's commitment to secure workplace roles in change without causing obstacles and disruption.

Acknowledging progress and successes as the change strategy moves forward communication rewards in a supporting manner that needs to be conveyed to the process and the workplace participants. Commending changes and keeping momentum charged places employee mentality at its best for participation in the process.

The success of teams that involve management and employees when change is happening should be a positive process for executing a plan. The team needs to know what is going on and feel comfortable with how it will transpire for success.

A simple guide to accountability needs vision and mission of the organization aligning it with the change process. The concept and purpose guides day-to-day events of everyone involved in the organization. When using the vision and mission protocol, make it easy, brief, and ready to recall. The organization's mantra needs to capture the very soul of the organization for how it will attain it's goal.

Setting up strategies, goals, objectives, and action plans (SGOAP) for change delves into identifying core values and best practices. There are statements (roadmap) that connect (SGOAP) to the vision and mission idea of the organization for purpose and success.

Looking at a strategizing direction (roadmap) commits you to planting a seed for growth and progression. A more in-depth look at approaching a strategy is how one uses a mission to succeed in one's vision. Procedures outline a foundational plan for getting at something purposeful. In this mode, an organization seeks creativity and is innovative in constructing and missioning a persistent idea.

The goals that are set up by an organization should focus on the direction to execute and complete for success. Setting up goals become a vital part of forming a strategy. Make sure the goals mirror the approach that represents where the plan is going. Limit setting your goals so not to gamble on the direction of the roadmap for completing. Also, plan your goals so that they don't oppose and impede with each other in addressing them. A goal should look at accomplishing an easy idea to understand. The plan requires completion and alignment to what value it brings to the organization and the workplace. An essential element to change entails flexibility as needed and involvement.

Thinking about setting up a clear objective brings about an idea of able time focused and measurable results. Objectives are quantifiable forms for a plan, fitting the goal of the program, check to see how likely the target is real, and the responsibility and commitment to completing the purpose. Action plans are detail actions or events used to attain a goal within the challenges of the objective.

In the end, it is the ownership on the part of the organization and its supporting cast of workplace participants that brings consensus to both collaborations in missioning participatory vision and input to completion.

WORKSHEET #8

List 10 examples of status quo challenges.

1. Asking questions like why certain things are done a certain way.

2. Offering remote work or flex times at a job that is typically done in person

3. More flexible scheduling

4. Taking EVERY perspective into account when asking for new ideas and before making decisions

5. Traditionally marginalized people (POC, LGBTQ+, etc.) being in positions of power/leadership positions

6. Finding methods of performing tasks that are more efficient than generally accepted practices

7. If employees consistently miss deadlines, suggest implementing a new way to track and manage tasks

8. Creating a more inclusive work environment

9. Taking advantage of new technology in order to implement new approaches

10. Being open to and committed to change, but especially positive change

CHAPTER 6
SCANNING THE COURT

© Kiki Dohmeier/Shutterstock.com

Leadership has many elements in being alert and competent in the workplace. It is in the organization and the "self" that being observant casts a certain savvy of awareness and alertness throughout the work and personal operational environment. We understand this to be known as an observant leader. Its skill looks at environmental awareness, alertness, being visible, and the need of "being there when you need to BE." "Scanning the court" opens up a useful venue as to how in touch the individual is in the leading environment. An observant leader's skill does not need to be used negatively nor positively but is purposeful in being savvy in the surroundings that embody the workplace environment.

If you are an observant leader, you focus on particulars in your surroundings. Sharp leaders pay attention to details that focus on image, appearance, colors, height, weight, conversation, etc., working to obtain this skill in working and preparing roles that can provide a heads up to forming a team. An observant leader learns to develop a vision that is both quick and specific, but one that can deliver gathered information for a purposeful plan.

A purposeful plan in the observant world pays attention to interpersonal issues and conflicts that may be cause for disrupting the strategy of the attentive leader's vision. It is how the workplace participants step up to address the challenge or if they are up to the task.

Observant leaders pay attention all the time. They have excellent listening skills and communicate clearly. They may use an investigative language approach without the obviousness of prying into personal manners, but they are excellent in preparing organization directions, roadmaps, and plans.

When this type of leader speaks of speed and details, it means they notice everything and their attention span covers all aspects of encounters with personnel and workplace environment.

Skill in an observant's possession is their effectiveness that have acquired both strands in action and delivery. The due date or deadline issue springs this leader into implementation and completion. The trust and dependency in this leadership presence are that they depend on others to be just as informed and quick to act, but this can be a fault in their possessive manner.

One of the most significant support mechanisms for the observant leader is critical thinking and detecting. They learn from their environments, both indoors and outdoors. Developing a skill for a sense of awareness or alertness comes from the affective domain, more focused on individual moods, demeanor, and presence. This leadership style does not ignore feelings and attitudes. It absorbs and develops them to their advantage. What is leadership by observation is that building an additive skill that attains differential worth in exercising sizing up of people. Being self-aware of people and surroundings is strength in reading individuals. Good leadership needs being best at observing. A leader who is observant has a skill that is further along than being self-aware. Knowing oneself as an observer is critical, but finding individuals attaining additional skills that are in tune with constructive engagement, work hand-in-hand, to keeping it real for yourself and individuals making a connection to a definite purpose.

A reasonable observer takes time to re-examine thy self and others. Observing harvests designs of perceptions on how the observant leader assesses recognition. In observation leadership, the beginning of placing one foot in front of the other to connect observation skill should begin here.

Elements of an observant leader in building balance come down to family, life, and the workplace environment. It is the goal of the leading individual to quantify time in addressing the three elements that can impact "scanning the court," being observant for the purposeful direction.

The conduct of leading by observation moves to understand the designs, the style, and the results for this leadership type. We see that the direction is to acquire the chief weapon of being better at awareness both in the self and the group. Being aware collaboratively brings about a collective standard of reading each other and understanding a working objective. When a leader shares purposeful leading designs a form of ideals emerge with the team member, and the goal or objective is to instill clarity for active participation. The style grows to be recognizable by the working group, being understanding and buying for useful input and unity at the working table. Separation from leader and worker is not what we want to feel but have contributory insights to the process. The result needs to create significant ways of exploring excellent and successful process.

Careful consideration when working with the rank and file is to define when one is observing or judging. It seems that when looking at something or someone, an observatory state prepares to express the image that is seen. In judging, one tends to direct a comment, conversation, opinion, and to show a feeling about something or someone that may draw a negative response or attitude.

What we learn is to pass judgment on individuals and the way they act in any given environment. The leaders need to check themselves because this is an excellent way to impact workplace productivity.

When feedback is evident the information delivered needs to be focused on positive, productive statements to individuals. Do not set up a climate where the defense or offense of individuals are set to play and reveal itself.

The impartial aspect of the process of judgment and observation can go haywire. Talking and thinking about levels of consideration need to bring out the neutral part of the understanding approach. Observations report image feedback for positive and constructive responses. It is essential to be more observant, and be able to deliver comments in a positive, constructive manner, which is crucial to provide communication, recommendations, and purposeful leading efficiently.

The strong part of working with peers is learning to read, understand, and relate to observant people. Being in tune to your surroundings can sometimes mean that they can anticipate and be ahead of others in "the thinking"; it can be an asset and so, a particular kind of cleverness can propel individuals in leadership and team-oriented coaching.

Some scouting points to recognize one as an observant leader can be how they conduct themselves and behave in the environment of leading people and relate to people.

Attention aptitude is an endurance trait that comes into play when observing in the environment of leading. This trait holds excellent stamina for finding possibilities and opportunities to put thought into the workplace environment.

A lot of times judging can be mistaken for making a call on someone or something on just mere observation. Being observant does not mean that you are accurate all the time but places one in a position of preparedness to execute a decision to a movement toward a goal. Something like a lie or a not so factual bit of information can indicate an approach to testing and evaluate situations and individuals. The strive for perfection in being on the money for dealing with people and issues are a motiving factor for being observant. Most observers do not want to be wrong or commit an error when pursuing a gut feeling that may throw off a potential advancement to being right. Observant people do not want to be wrong because their self-worth strength depends on it. Observation can teach and be a learning tool at the same time. What observant leaders want to accomplish is being cohesive and directive to set goals and objectives that follow their scouting report and finding to execute team and individual greatness.

Develop a Venn diagram of your observant skills.

Venn Diagram   Name _____

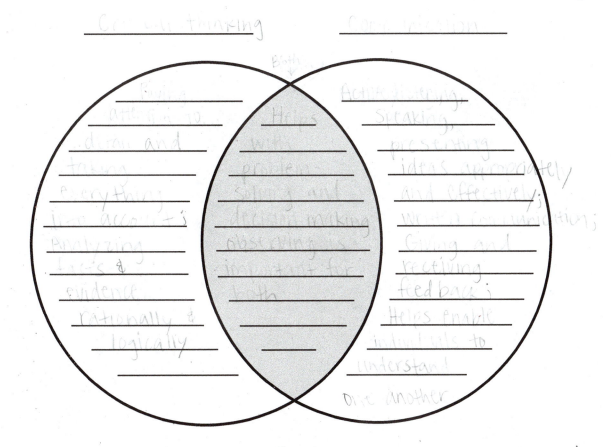

Critical thinking   Communication

Giving attention to detail and taking everything into account; Analyzing facts & evidence rationally & logically

Both

Helps with problem-solving and decision making; observing is important for both

Active listening, speaking, presenting ideas appropriately and effectively; written communication; Giving and receiving feedback; Helps enable individuals to understand one another

CHAPTER 7
FOURTH QUARTER LEADERSHIP

© FloridaStock/Shutterstock.com

B eing a fourth quarter leader brings about competitive superiority and effectiveness in experiencing success and taking on the opposition, the unknown, "fear."

Defining competitive superiority is reaching a stance of being there when you have to "BE." Situations occur and "callouts" exist in dealing with the environment of people and work every day, every moment, to meet the needs and address issues.

True competitive superiority is taken on when a challenging situation needs to be dealt with. It is this time that organization preparation directs tackling issue with glee. Handling adversity and getting purpose of it come from the attitude that the leader puts forth. Time to take on matters brings about desire to stream through this dealing with difficulty, whereas you, as a leader, can be head on with something unique somewhat in an ordinary situation. There is no learning and development in simple cases to ease; it is when situations present uneasiness that we learn and put into the experience bank. This part of leading describes how a leader can show approach of example toward being a competitive leader. The thought here is, as it gets rough, how rough can you be?

Competitive superiority packages itself in not being hesitant to take on a battle for the good and being able, of being there, when you have to "BE." Sometimes a leader may gain success by taking on a situation and being called lucky. But luck in leadership is known as luck that results from planning to encounter chance.

Elements of a fourth quarter leader need to be foundationally solid in its appearance and delivery. There are eight connectors to being a fourth quarter leader.

Planning is essential to the fourth quarter leader in that it cognitively seeks the strategic aspect of thinking and planning for fourth quarter leadership. This leader needs to be a mediator in bringing issues, introducing boundaries, organizing opinions and input into a collective purposeful direction. One connector that is assumed from the floor is that this individual in the area of leadership is a diplomat. Now, exercising diplomacy is an art form that not just anyone can exhibit. A diplomat is someone who uses tact, managerial skills, people person, and dealing with situations that are often fragile in nature. One of the most needed strengths in being a fourth quarter leader is being a team builder. Team building is the means of turning a unit of individuals into a unified team, interconnecting people to work together on their skill, and collectively achieving purpose and results. This individual needs to have a gift of being transparent and able to communicate to the fullest. Exercising excellent communication skills in the work environment is all about being able to be clear and direct to individuals, in a manner that clarifies information for understanding and project completion. This leader finds the human part of empathy and respect to deliver sound leadership. It brings about character representation in being considerate of others. This leadership focus in the area of productivity works to demonstrate direction in the path of having protocol, process, and productivity objectives and goals for purposeful results. The fourth quarter is a finisher and project completion. The leader represents a scenario that speaks to, if there is 3 seconds in the fourth quarter of a game left, what are you going to do? Pass it or shoot? A fourth quarter leader knows what to do. This leader will be a closer in the areas of problems, encounters, meeting goals and objectives, purposeful tasks, and human dignity.

Understanding what a fourth quarter leader contributes to image and personality of this leading mentality includes attributes that fulfill shaping leadership cause from leading individuals.

The areas that reinforce purposeful leadership in individual's display is how they are implemented, their attitudes, passion, and competitive superiority. The three attributing factors that drive and provide thinking, feeling, and finishing for goals and objectives are attributes that enable and bring belief to strategic success.

It is essential that purposeful leadership be in machine form fitness wise to ensure balancing of the mind and body. The decision-making process of projects and of people need to be supported by leaders who are sound in healthy pondering and unveiling of productive ideas. In addition, the maintenance of stamina and endurance in body balance bring about stabilizing vision to mission purposeful organization and workplace competitive execution.

Building team and organizing a culture for success come from the treatment of individuals. Two elements come to mind in a genuine consideration and cooperation for others. Leaders shape and recruit members to fit roles and construct a game plan. The important part on how each participant is able to accept the contributory assignment to fulfill by input and by commitment results in winning and success coming out of team efforts that each participant gave. Time is an additive for pacing and focusing on the prize. Modeling relationship connections in building teams add to success for effectiveness, respect, and dignity. Individuals need to know that they are valued and preparing to be part of a group that is out to do great things.

The influence that a fourth quarter leader exhibits on looking into the future keeps it real and genuine to set no limitations for success.

Fourth quarter preparation and organization are two elements in working with people supporting and placing direction and ideas on the table for a transparent plan for group success. How leaders communicate and listen to others tells a lot of about the influencing factors that bring about effective and constructive project comprehension. Opportunity for participants should be encouraged for development to acquire group experience. This can be an asset in bringing about determination to complete. Again, uniting respect, trustworthiness, time on hand forms seeing the end result to fruition. Fourth quarter leadership offers team participants to seek challenges for experiential acquisition and knowledge. Fourth quarter leadership welcomes this information back to the group. Teams and organizations find competitive superiority by effective planning to achieve a high level of competency.

A fourth quarter leader establishes a model delivering essential influential factors that balance the floor for treatment of leadership team, strategic value for purpose, and awareness of components in community of people, organizational cultures, and change for missioning vision:

4TH QUARTER LEADERSHIP WEB

Empower the Community   **Motivate the Community**

4th Quarter Leadership

Lead Positive Social Change   **Missioning a Vision**